Introduction

In a wedding, it is normally the bride who takes the spotlight—the only woman whom all eyes are open to behold. Her choice of gown for making her appearance to the groom and guests will determine a dull or bright wedding. Whether she will be talked of as a banal, unengaging figure strolling the aisle or an enthusing and breath-taking queen is really up to one thing---the wedding dress.

But before taking you on the tour of what best to choose and wear as the wife-to-be, we must first pass through some other significant considerations regarding wedding dresses.

Colours

The best colours for wedding dresses in the western world are pink, cream and white. These colours are bright. The bride should look lively on her special day. Pink, cream or white offers that comfortable in-between where the colours are not too bright and not dull. A too bright colour would be yellow. A too dull—or rather disastrous-- colour would be black.

If you live in the Middle East, other colours may be more popular.

Length

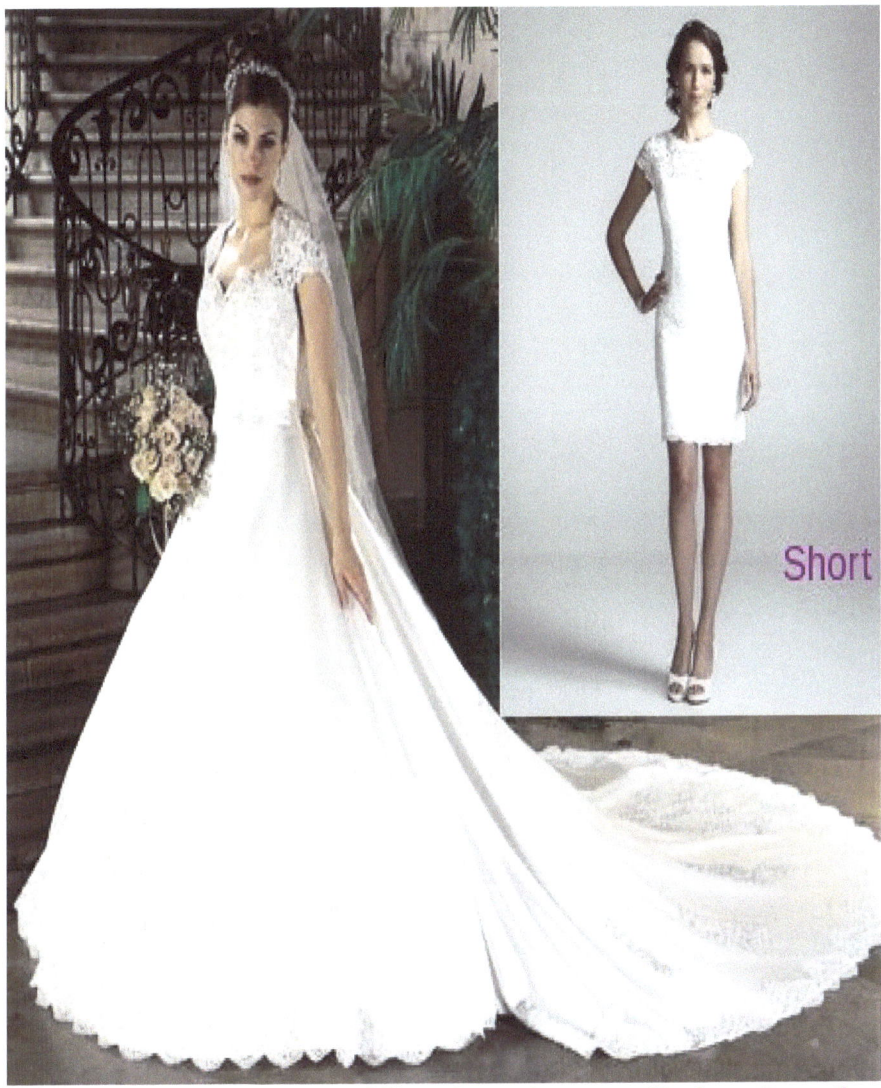

The length of the wedding dress is normally based on the personal taste of the bride and, where allowed, the groom. But the length should also be decided according to the age of the bride. The older the bride---age 50 or over—the less length there should be at the bottom of the dress.

Headpiece

The headpiece can be done in any of many designs. This headpiece was done without the veil or a band, suitable only for the bride with lots of hair. It is multi-purpose and therefore can be worn on other occasions.

Every wedding dress should be worn with a headpiece. How large or small the headpiece will be, and the design of it, will depend a lot on the taste of the bride. Her coiffure will also play into her decision. If the bride's hair is very short—or if she has no hair—a headpiece made with a band would be the best choice. The band is the part of the headpiece that will hold it in place. The bride with lots of hair, on the other hand, has the option of choosing a headpiece with or without band.

It is not a good idea to mix colours into the headpiece. A lot of colours on top the bride's head is simply ridiculous and confusing. In fact, this may create a childish look. If there is a desire to add colours to the headpiece, the maximum amount should be two— example: white and pink.

The wedding dress also plays into the choice of headpiece. The colour of the wedding dress determines the colour of the headpiece. Both should match.

The Veil

The veil is still an embellishing element to the headpiece and can be done in any of many designs. The best colour for the bridal veil is pink or white.

The headpiece can be made with or without a veil. Though excluded from many headpieces worn nowadays, the veil still has the undiminishing ability to ennoble and glamourize the bride. These days, the veil is fashioned on many headpieces so that it does not carry that old-time or bygone look.

Some brides choose to wear hats instead. But hats, importantly, are more fitting to the older brides. A young bride wearing a hat as her headpiece would most likely be considered old-fashion in many societies today.

The bouquet

The bouquet (pronounced **boo-kay**) is an intrinsic accessory to the bride. The bride—even in a nude wedding—must be accompanied by the bouquet. The bouquet is not just a bunch of flowers. Like the headpiece, the bouquet is a compulsory accessory for the bride. It's an element of the bride's appearance which carries rules.

Rule one: The colour of the bouquet must be opposite to the colour of the bride's dress. This is necessary so that the bouquet stands out from the dress. If the dress is white and the bouquet is white, for example, there won't be much visibility of the bouquet, especially in video and photographs.

Rule two: The bouquet should not consist of one colour but a mixture of colours. You can use one colour throughout, but you should at least differ in the colour of the ribbon used to wrap the petals together.

Rule three: The bride's bouquet should look different from the ones to be carried by the bridesmaids.

The dress and the bride's body

The wedding dress should be chosen for the bride and not the bride for the wedding dress. In other words, the body type (size, height and shape) of the bride must be used to decide the style dress that best suites her—instead of first finding a dress of a gorgeous style and try to fit it on the bride. Some dress styles do not go well with some body types.

It is not the dress that will shape the bride's body. It is the bride's body that will shape the dress.

Chapter One

Wedding dresses for brides 18-45

This may not be the perfect choice for the bride under age 30.

A headpiece with veil is most fitting for this gown

The mermaid design is most fitting for the bride with broad hip.

Chapter Two

Wedding Dresses for the bridge 45 or older

The *posture of the model is terrible,* but *the dress is not*

Photos of
Majority wedding dresses
From
Brides.com

Nigel D. Salmon is an author. He lives in St Elizabeth, Jamaica.

Website: www.NigeldSalmon.com